HOW TO START ANY BUSINESS AND GET JOBS

Self-employment: a beginner's guide

Welcome!

This write-up is of four dimensions, all of them channeling you into becoming that person you want to be, the successful business young man or lady with practical steps.

The first dimension is

> Your talents and your passions

The second dimension is

> Business start-up

The third dimension is

> Jobs start-up

The fourth dimension

The first Dimension

Your talents and your passions

I would like to unwrap to you the wonders people mine from their talents and passions with the title...

YOUR PASSION CAN BE YOUR NEXT JOB

You may have heard of Dickens Charles, a famous writer in 1827 from London, England. He never knew his passion could make him famous until he delved into it. When his father was sent to prison, there was a financial struggle in the family. He got a work of gluing labels on bottles in a factory and he hated it. Charles Dickens was intelligent and ambitious but he did not know where to channel his talent. He was discouraged in the factory because it is a job made for the illiterate and dirty. Charles saved some money while working so he figured out what to do. In the British Museum he spent hours studying, he discovered a profession that he is passionate with which is journalism.it appealed to his love of literature and the decision to become a Journalist was a surprise to his family members and they did not believe he would succeed because they thought it will be too big for him. When Charles

reached twenty –one, he was considered to be the most rapid, the accurate

and the most trustworthy reporter then on the London press. He said he has

talent in craft and writing, so he was developing more and practicing

constantly moving into becoming a professional author. The more he wrote

for magazine even for free, the more he sharpened his talent. When Charles

Dickens was twenty-five years, his Novel; pickwick sold 1.6 million copies.

Let your Passion be in action

You said you have passion for something, let us see your actions towards that. Whether you are weak or strong, there must be something you love just like we fall in love or admire somebody with all our hearts.

The active force of passion makes people elected. I tell people that wherever their own craziness lies, just make it well known. It's just passion in action. In higher institutions, some lecturers are crazy with their passions in teaching, once they see crowd of students, they feel like dancing. They knew they can make people laugh and they also aware of possessing a great passion for lecturing. They decided to follow a specific path and they are giving in their best. So you cannot carry everything along. Just because you have love for acting, dancing, cooking, driving, teaching and other things does not mean that you should look for job in all of them. And many people because they cannot choose one or two and concentrate, each day they sit in open places thinking, and flicking their legs left and right as if they want to run away or that the legs are hot. What is happening in their heads are also happening in their legs. Say passion, when you hear these words, harden not your heart as you did in other books. Passion for something will make you elected and act crazy about that which you love doing and that's when people will begin to clap for you. People's needs make us productive and busy trying to find a solution. It must touch your heart, occupy your emotions and you must bear a reward of applause in your mind when you find the solution, and this is motivation.

You can remember Aristotle and the wisdom seeking young man. Until you desire wisdom like you would gasps for air you will not get it. The great philosopher taught him to gasps for wisdom like he would gasps for air when his head is in the water. So also until passion grows into a strong necessity like breathing and people notice it, that person will not change level. Passion is the motivator for strong actions, anybody that is passionate for something knows the reward from that which he is passionate for. That is why people persist in something, if they fall they rise because they know passion has reward. Steve Jobs said "I'm convinced that the only thing that kept me going was that I loved what I did, you have got to find what you love". When you talk about talented people, all of them noticed their passion for that which they do and they kept doing it.

Human resource managers and employers are looking for passion oriented applicants (talents)

Ronaldo, Messy, Kalu, and many others love football (passion) and they are talented. Michael Jackson, Jay Z, Davido, Rihanna, Eminem, Phyno and many others love music and are crazy about it (passion) and they are talented. Chinua Achebe of things fall apart, Joyce Meyer, Alice Seybold, Wole Soyinka, Jeff Unegbu a great voluminous biography writer and many others love writing (passion) and they are talented. Great scholars, golfers, wrestlers, actors, mathematicians, doctors, engineers, speakers, preachers, fighters, teachers, coaches, and many others in different areas love what they are doing and they are talented. These people discovered their passion for something, acted immediately and are showing their talents.

In every Curriculum Vitae commonly known as CV, every human resource manager will always want to see proves for the appended skills and hobbies. Where everyone is qualified, not everyone can be employed so they look for what an applicant has as an edge over others. Imagine if you have worked for people on power point presentation which is a computer skill, and you list the company or individuals you have worked for, they will be impressed. It will show them that you have passion for computer and it has made you go extra mile and on the verge to becoming talented. The only way to show passion is the level of practice which leads to advancement in that skill. Job recruiters want to see your advancement in the skills you possess if not you have left it long ago. Okay what is the evidence of your problem solving skill? Or what complex issue have you contributed in giving a solution to? Maybe in hobbies, a tennis player who proclaims himself a good one should have engaged in trophies. Or you have reading as your hobby therefore you love it, you should also include a quick evidence that you are a prolific reader. A prolific reader should be a great writer and engages in competitions. If you engage in frequent reading, you should also engage in conducting researches and submit to a related association. Or write books for others to read and by so doing you are already busy. Maybe you included singing and dancing in your hobbies, you should also have engaged in any competition no matter how small or local the competition may be. You may also have young people you work with or train, when you do so, people will notice your passion. Skills without evidence is a prove of unskillfulness. If there is no evidence for the skills in your curriculum vitae that means you don't have the skills. Passion oriented job applicants improve on their skills and hobbies, that is an essential tool for the job you are seeking. So next time you are applying for a job, make sure you always include any evidence or advancement you have on your skills and hobbies, job recruiters will be impressed to meet a talented and a celebrity you are.

Thanks! thanks!! thanks!!!

Business start-up

Look for something in high demand that you can do

Meet people that are into it

Be an obedient apprentice or student

Establish your own through your master

Register your business

Manage your business

Make an edge over your competitors

Reinvest your gain for expansion.

Self-employment is a condition whereby someone is in charge or controls his or her own source of income or business venture. He or she can be a business owner who sells physical products or renders service, a contractor, or a consultant who renders services. Self-employment means that you are your own boss in a particular business or any source of income, so you decide when to start and when to close. In the business language, self-employment is a business venture because the owner is busy daily doing what can be seen and understood by a set of the population he or she chooses and it is that which yields profit.

What is business? Scholars in the area like Brown and Petrella (1979), defined it as any organized effort to produce products or supply services demanded by people for the purpose of making profit. The key words there are- products and service, demand and profit making. Because people want to shave their bears, dye their hairs any colour they want, dread their hair and cut their hair any style they wish so that they look cute and presentable, some guys met experts to learn such skills and today they are doing well. They rendering the services and making profits. They are self employed and managers. Many of them sell clippers, dyes, inner wears for guys, show case wrist watches and other items for guys in the same barbing shop. So they combined rendering services and selling products.

A brother who repairs phones has also copied and replicated the idea and its working for him; rendering services and also selling products. Like in most barbing salons, if you enter his shop, you sit and watch movies and cable programs while he repairs your phone. He is now selling products like mobile phones, chargers and accessories. When he was beginning, he had no television and he rendered just services but today he has expanded to the extent of training others. So he is now a service provider and a business man at 27. Maybe in the next ten years or less if he continues with the same spirit of entrepreneurship, he will own a warehouse of phone parts and phone shops in different locations.

Self- employment is a form of sole proprietorship and sole proprietorship according to Chiaka Obi is a business owned and managed by one man. A self-employed person enjoys these privileges

Owns his profit

Decides how to run his business

Has close supervision on his business

He has no committee to argue with (freedom of action)

He is not expected to pay special taxes and so on.

Note

A self-employed person is a business owner that was under someone who is superior to him in the business training and coaching him for a specified period of time.

He or she does not disengage completely from his boss because a boss has more help and advice to offer.

Every self-employed who just began his own purchases goods through his boss

Every apprentice, that is a job or business learner is not left after his apprenticeship unless the fellow decides to go his way or change business. So don't be afraid if you want to learn business.

A self-employed person can be a business owner who sells products and services or a contractor or a consultant for an example a drug vendor sells products, a building contractor gets contracts and renders services, a wielder

Jobs start-up

Practical steps to getting started as a contractor

Now that you are a skilled builder or architect, for you to start up and execute contracts confidently and correctly, you have to work under an expert who is your boss, through him you will be known and get your own contract.

If you are trained by a professor who is not in the practical line, after your studies or during break times you join those in the practical line as a labourer. Introduce yourself and your discipline, when they notice your skills, they will like to work with you. You must serve before you become a boss.

Some students assume that once they graduate from higher institutions they are already masters, what of those that have stayed in the field for ten, twenty and thirty years?

Practical examples

Mr. B. was a second year student in a polytechnic, he noticed that uncles, and brothers are building and renovating their homes in the village, he quickly made two changes in his career pursuit he did not regret. He quickly changed his course of study to architecture, secondly he purchased some items for building work such s shovels, head pans, measuring tapes, and line. He joined builders s a labourer, they were teaching him and he was also learning in school, he even financed his studies. Today mr. a is a builder who uses Archi card in drawing. He now builds houses for his uncles, brothers, friends, church members and other clients. So today he is a building contractor.

Another young man also utilized a similar observation and changed his life. The business of waste recycling; this a business that one can start instantly and I am going to tell how my neighbor began.

Mr. C was a very successful and happy young man in his job in Port Harcourt city Nigeria. He got retrenched from the job and was idle. One afternoon, he noticed some people picking pure water sachets. More enquiries made him to understand that those people pick the sachets, pack them in big bags and sell to industries that will recycle them. Mr. C is a tall and handsome man, living in a good apartment but when he noticed he could not stay idle anymore, he picked up the job that is available and lucrative.

Waste recycling is under the ministry of health and environment. So a person doing may be working for the government. People package their jobs in romantic names so that ones you hear it, a high profile personality will come into your mind. That is why road side mechanics that stopped at primary and secondary school call themselves engineers and drug sellers prefer to be addressed as doctors. Waste management in everywhere in the world involves a safe collection of wastes to a designated place. An interest in waste management job can lead one into meeting companies in like; universal care ltd (ucl) in Lagos Nigeria, waste point ldt, Fedoz Nigeria ltd in Port Harcourt and so on.

Scaffolding jobs

Mr. D is a Bsc. Holder in computer engineering who spent a long period of time doing job he did not like. Mr. D being a Nigerian knew that an engineer can venture into any engineering work and excel. So he enrolled in learning scaffolding and job safety (HSE) after getting the skills, he approached a civil engineer who gets contracts and looks for workers. The civil engineer accommodated him and began to give him even supervisory jobs as an engineer.

Summary of his steps

Mr D graduated as a computer engineer

Got additional skill as an edge

Met an engineer who goes to the field

Secures contracts.

He positioned himself as a common scaffolder and his expertice and trustworthiness paved way for him into becoming a contractor. He took action and made a good conversation with the civil engineer.

Job and business seekers' watch words

- Every job seeker wants the job at the spot; it is by God's grace they accept 'we will get back to you'. Author

- Job seekers are always in a hurry, often neglecting start-up jobs around them. A story is told of one who abandoned their family's drink selling shops for another family's company. A shop he can grow into a company if he is a real entrepreneur. Author

- "Nothing in the world can take the place of persistence, talents will not, nothing is more common than unsuccessful men with talents, genius will not, unrewarded genius is almost a proverb, education will not, the world is full of educated derelicts, persistence and determination alone are omnipotent, the slogan press on has solved and will always solve the problems of human race"- Calvin Coolidge, the thirtieth president of the united states from 1923 to 1929.

- "When you leave college, there will be thousands of people with the same degree you have. When you get a job, there will be thousands doing what want to do for a living. But you are the only person alive who has sole custody of your life"- Anna Quindlen, an American author.

- Every job seeker should know that technology is advancing and there is a call for more advanced technological knowledge and as Jonathan Grudin puts it 'technology is already central and it will undoubtedly play greater role in the years ahead'. Jonathan Grudin is a principal design researcher at micro soft.

- Anybody that is so dearly in need of something and ruminates it in his mind, will begin to notice opportunities in the environment.

- A good business man must have nose for business the same way a journalist has nose for news. In places where people see obstacle, I see a lot of opportunities. A good business man sees where others don't see. Orji Uzor Kalu, a business man and former Governor of Abia state Nigeria.

- Jared Goetz a digital marketer and author of e-Commerce Hacks courses wrote on his Facebook timeline how scooters became a trend in San Diego in 2016. Vander Zandan bought brand new bikes for his two daughters, to his surprise, they prefer their old scooters because scooters would provide more fun, but scooters were not fun for adults. Vander Zandan thought of adding motor to scooters. He decided to order a power scooter from China and tried it out. Him and his wife went riding around San Diego, people were interested and desired to have one each. According to Jared Goetz, the idea for bird scooters was instantly born and today, Bird is a big company worth billions of dollars. Jared Goetz called this 'finding opportunity in an obvious place'. He encourages people to train themselves to take chances if they want to be great entrepreneurs. Jared said 'keep your eyes open, look for opportunities wherever you go'.

- Now as you graduate to begin anew, I wish that for you, 'stay hungry, stay foolish'. Steve Jobs co-founder of Apple inc.

- It doesn't make sense to hire smart people and tell them what to do; we hire smart people so they tell us what to do. Steve Jobs. It is only those who have followed up a company for a long time or who read the historical progress and lapses can tell what to do. You can also use hash tags to get insider information.

- The best way to sell something- don't sell anything. Earn the awareness, respect and trust of those who might buy. Rand Frankish, a CEO and co-founder of search engine optimization in moz software company in 2004.

- The consumer is not a moron; she is your wife. David Ogilvy, the father of advertising from England. He researched so much on consumer habits.

- Empathy, focus, and impute were the three goals of the initial 'Apple marketing philosophy'. Apple was built from the heart. Steve jobs.

- Many candidates get over looked because of previous mistakes. It caused their resumes to be less than ideal. John Tolan, the CEO of spark hires. Be careful what you state in your resume.

- If you hear a voice within say "you cannot paint". Then by all means paint and that voice will be silenced. Vincent Van Gogh, a Dutch famous painter.

- Whenever you are asked if you can do a job, tell them 'certainly I can' then get busy and find out how to do it. Theodore Roosevelt, the 26th president of the United States from 1901 to 1909

- Present yourself both in person and online, in a polished and professional way.

- Today's job seekers should have an online presence in social media, where they showcase their skills and experiences and they must be the same in all the social media they sign in. Alison Doyle, a United States' job search expert.

- Every job seeker should be careful what he shoot online in different social media, because there talents are hunt, accessed and may be dropped. Author

- One of the smarter ways to start work after college or university studies is to invest in your passion. Alison Doyle calls it turning your hobby into a career. Hobbies for example bead making, that person can get more trainings on jewelry designing. The person will someday produce, sell and teach others. A love for researching can land one into assistant researcher to an academia in a school, journalism or book and article writing and publishing. A love for cooking can make one a caterer or event manager.

- A love for entrepreneurship makes one a business owner. A love for singing may make one a ceremonial musician in live music who will eventually become a recorded artist. You can write us to help you with your passion

- To job hunters and workers, always know that managers and bosses are using tweets, instagram, Facebook and other social media so comment carefully. Google has also facilitated their search.

- When everything seems to be going against you, remember that the airplane takes off against the wind, not with it. Henry Ford, the founder of Ford motor company in America.

- There is good news; companies that do not entertain mediocre offer merit-based employment, so job seekers should not lose hope.

Job seekers should prepare for questions that employers ask to find out if the candidate researched the company before applying and coming for interview. Questions like-job specification and role, the products, values and visions of the company. they are usually found on the company's website.

Changing jobs

Job hopping has made job employers and recruiters ask job applicants during interviews what their career goals could be. Getting jobs and quitting them and looking for another one could be a long hill for job seekers. John Tolen, the CEO of spark Hires aired a great view point when he said "job hoppers are an employer's nightmare, many believe evidence of job hopping on a resume is a big red flag against hiring the candidate. So job seekers get passed over because its assumed they will just quit the job as well".

Here, we are concerned with how to successfully get a new job with the number of previous jobs listed in the resume and also what your dream career could be to avoid future frustrations in an undesired job position.

Well, trying to merge passion and career, job hopping is vital until you get your choice especially if you are young and in a state or region where there are many job opportunities. In some countries, people are begging for any available job and their salaries are poor and some talents there are waste of time. They keep migrating to better states and countries.

According to Confucious the great Greek Philosopher 2000 or more years ago "choose a job you love and you will never have to work a day in your life". Some job seekers will say don't worry, but Confucious was talking about job and satisfaction. It is fun and makes people remain healthy, because they are doing a job they put in their skills and talents empathically they don't feel like been forced to work but rather living their lives. People like this when you meet them coming back from work and you shout praise the lord, they will joyfully shout Alleluia and add God is good.

Before people begin to think of changing their jobs, they must have discovered better opportunities or where they will express their skills or where they think is better for them depending on their reasons; maybe a wrong admirer in the same office. Young people change jobs for little reason. For instance a young man suddenly jammed huge money so he decided to quit his job in a company because his level changed. Because of his wealth, colleagues that were helpful to him became enemies. So he moved on in luxury life. While he Was enjoying, government investigators were looking for him everywhere. They got him, prosecuted him, he stayed in jail, was released and headed to regain him position in the company. When the manager saw him in his office his insult was worse than calling security on him. He drove him out and told him 'you are finished, in fact you are dead and buried long ago, you want to terminate my company the way you just terminated your life.

People also change job because of late payment of salary and in most cases the salary is poor. People also change job to make more connections with others and also for job satisfaction.

References

Brown, D.R, and Petrello, G.J. (1970). Introduction to Business (2nd ed), Califonia: publishing co.ink

Chiaka Obi (2011). Elements of business. De- verge agencies ltd, p.11